How Do They Grow?

From Kitten to Cat

by Jillian Powell

RAINTREE
STECK-VAUGHN
PUBLISHERS

A Harcourt Company

Austin   New York
www.steck-vaughn.com

Published by Raintree Steck-Vaughn Publishers, an imprint of Steck-Vaughn Company

Library of Congress Cataloging-in-Publication Data
Powell, Jillian.
From kitten to cat / by Jillian Powell.
    p.   cm.—(How do they grow?)
    Includes bibliographical references and index.
    ISBN 0-7398-4424-5
    1. Kittens—Juvenile literature. 2. Cats—Development—
Juvenile literature. [1. Cats. 2. Animals—Infancy. 3. Pets.]
I. Title.

SF445.7 P69   2001
638.8'07—dc21   00-054295

Printed in Italy. Bound in the United States.
1 2 3 4 5 6 7 8 9 0 05 04 03 02 01

Picture acknowledgments
Angela Hampton Family Life Picture Library 14, 17, 20, 21, 22, 23, 24, 25, 26, 28; NHPA 11; HWPL title page, 19; Gettyone Stone 29; Oxford Scientific Films 4 (F.Cicogna/Overseas), 5 (Herbert Schwind/ Okapia), 7 (Herbert Schwind/Okapia), 8 (G.I. Bernard), 15 (Marianne Wilding); RSPCA Photolibrary 6 (Ken McKay), 9 (Angela Hampton), 10 (Colin Seddon), 12 (Angela Hampton), 13 (Alan Robinson), 16 (Angela Hampton), 18 (Geoff du Feu), 27 (Geoff du Feu).

Contents

Words in **bold** in the text can be found in the glossary on page 30.

A Cat Gives Birth

This cat is giving birth to kittens. The first
kitten has just been born.

There are four kittens in this **litter**.

They are tiny and wet. The mother is tired.

She sleeps with her kittens.

Newborn Kittens

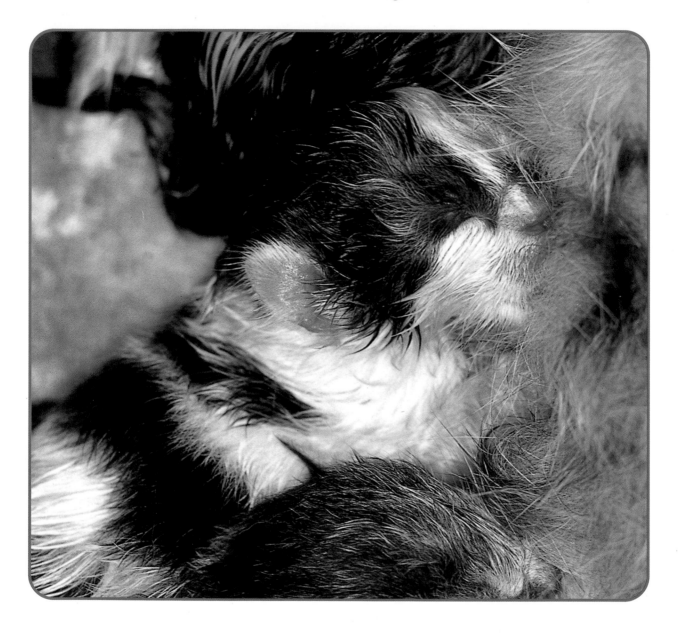

The mother feeds her kittens with her milk. The milk helps them grow strong and fight off **germs**.

The kittens snuggle close to their mother to keep warm. After feeding, some of the kittens fall asleep.

The First Few Days

For a few days, the kittens just sleep
and drink milk. Their mother keeps them
clean and warm.

These kittens are a week old. They cannot yet open their eyes. Their legs are floppy and weak. They wiggle around.

Getting Bigger

This kitten is two weeks old. Its eyes are now open, and it can see. Fur is growing on its ears and nose.

This kitten can now stand up, since its legs are growing stronger. Its legs are still wobbly when it tries to walk.

Becoming Playful

This kitten is three weeks old. It can walk and run around. Now the kitten wants to play.

The kitten learns to jump and **pounce** and use its paws and claws. It likes to chase and catch toys as if it is **hunting** mice.

13

Feeding and Keeping Clean

When they are four weeks old, the kittens grow
their first teeth. They can start
to eat kitten food.

This kitten can **groom** itself. It licks its paw to wash its face. The kitten keeps its fur clean by licking it all over.

Ready for a New Home

This kitten is growing fast. It will soon be ready
to leave its mother and go to a
new home.

When a kitten is over eight weeks old, it is ready to go to a new owner. The kitten needs to be handled gently so it feels safe.

Staying Indoors

The kitten must stay indoors until it is
12 weeks old. This keeps it safe from germs.

The vet checks that the kitten is healthy.
He gives it **vaccinations** to fight diseases.

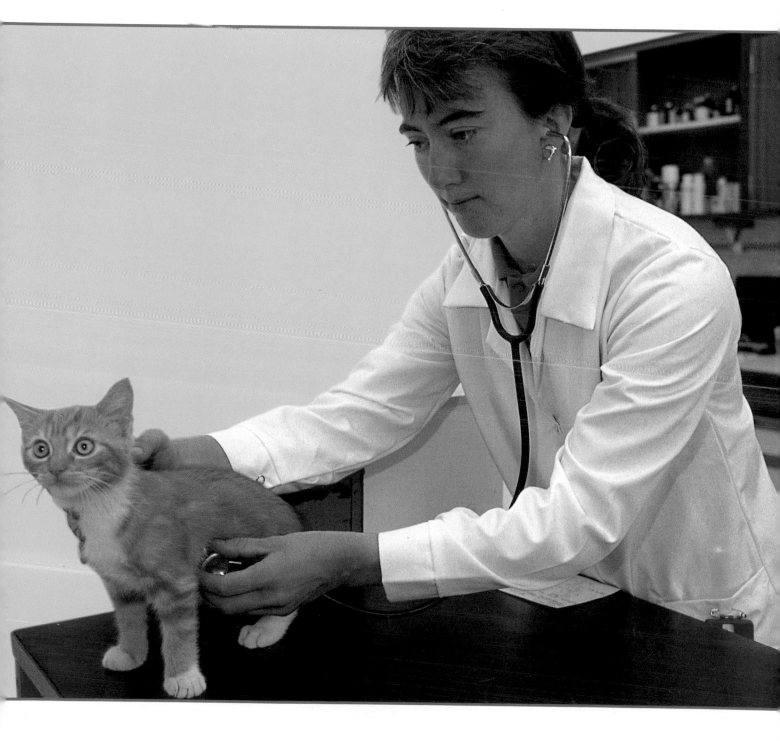

Keeping a Healthy Coat

The kitten feels safe and happy in its new home. It washes itself every day to keep clean.

The new owner grooms the kitten twice a week.
This brushes out the old fur, which the kitten
might swallow.

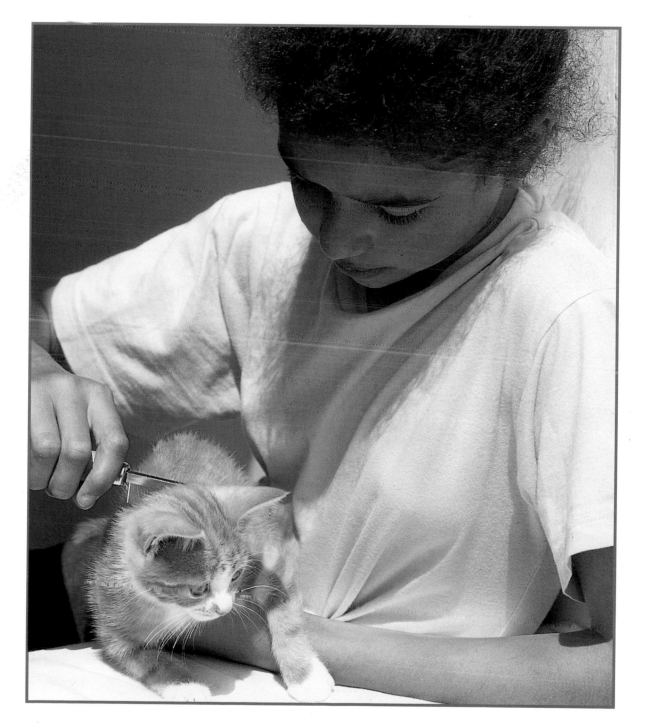

Scratching and Rubbing

A cat uses its claws to dig, to climb, and to hold on. It uses a **scratching post** indoors to sharpen its claws.

Outside, a kitten can sharpen its claws on trees. Cats leave a **scent** on trees that tells other cats where they have been.

Eating and Playing

A kitten eats three or four small meals every day.
The kitten food helps it grow bigger
and stronger.

The kitten loves to play. It plays with toys that teach it to chase and catch.

Exploring and Climbing

The kitten likes to explore. Its long whiskers help it measure spaces. Its eyes can see well even when it is dark.

The kitten has grown into a young cat. Its legs are long and strong, and it can jump and climb. Its tail helps it to balance.

Having Kittens

This cat is fully grown. She has **mated** with a **male** cat. Kittens have begun to grow inside her.

After the kittens are born, the cat will feed, wash, and look after them. Each kitten will grow up to be a strong, healthy cat.

Glossary

Germs (jurmz) Tiny particles around us that can carry diseases.

Groom (groomd) To keep an animal's fur clean.

Hunting (HUNT-ing) Chasing after another animal for food.

Litter (LIT-ur) All the young animals born to the same mother at the same time.

Male The opposite sex to female. The male is able to father babies. A female is able to become a mother.

Mated (MAY-ted) When a male and female have come together to have babies.

Pounce (pounss) jump on something suddenly.

Scent (sent) An animal's smell.

Scratching post (SKRACH-ing pohst) A specially made object that a cat can use to sharpen its claws.

Vaccinations (VAC-suh-nay-shuns) Injections given with a needle into the skin. These protect animals and people from diseases.

Further Information

Books

Doudna, Kelly. *Kittens*. Sandcastle, 2000.

Frost, Helen. *Cats*. Pebble Books, 2000.

Gibbons, Gail. *Cats*. Holiday House, 1996.

Head, Honor. *Kitten*. Raintree Steck-Vaughn, 2000.

Hinds, Kathryn. *Cats*. Marshall Cavendish, 1998.

Starke, Katherine. *Cats & Kittens*. EDC Publications, 1998.

Vrbova, Zuza. *Kittens*. Chelsea House, 1998.

Websites

www.aspca.org

The official site of the American Society for the Prevention of Cruelty to Animals (ASPCA), with lots of useful information on pet care.

www.lurch.net/pets.htm

A site which gives you advice about how to care for your pet. It also includes pages on the care of your cat plus games, stories and crafts.

Useful addresses

American Society for the Prevention of Cruelty to Animals
424 East 92nd Street, 4th Floor
New York, NY 10128-6804

Index

B

balancing 27

C

chasing 13, 25

cleaning 15, 20

D

diseases 19

E

exploring 26

eyes 9, 10, 26

F

food 14, 24, 29

fur 10, 15, 21

G

germs 6, 18

grooming 15, 21

H

hunting 13

M

mating 28

milk 6, 8

P

playing 12, 25

pouncing 13

S

safety 17

scent 23

scratching 22

sleeping 5, 7, 8

T

tail 27

teeth 14

toys 13, 25

V

vaccinations 19

vet 19

W

walking 11

washing 20, 29

whiskers 26